D1511135

Why can't I... Why can't I... Why can't I...
Can't I... Why can't I... Why can't I... Wh
I... Why can't I... Why can't I... Why can
Why can't I... Why can't I... Why can't I
Can't I... Why can't I... Why can't I... Why
I... Why can't I... Why can't I... Why can
Why can't I... Why can't I... Why can't I...
Can't I... Why can't I... Why can't I... Why
I... Why can't I... Why can't I... Why can
Why can't I... Why can't I... Why can't I...
Can't I... Why can't I... Why can't I... Why
I... Why can't I... Why can't I... Why can
Why can't I... Why can't I... Why can't 2

# Why can't I...

# take my plant for a walk?

### and other questions

### about plants

# Why can't I...

# take my plant for a walk?

## and other questions

## about plants

**Ruth Thomson**

Thameside Press

Distributed in the United States by
Smart Apple Media
1980 Lookout Drive
North Mankato, MN 56003

Text copyright © Ruth Thomson 2001

Editor: Claire Edwards
Designer: Jacqueline Palmer
Picture researcher: Diana Morris
Consultant: Anne Goldsworthy

Printed in Hong Kong

9  8  7  6  5  4  3  2  1

**Library of Congress Cataloging-in-Publication Data**

Thomson, Ruth.
    Take my plant for a walk? / written by Ruth Thomson.
        p.  cm. -- (Why can't I)
    Includes index.
    ISBN 1-930643-02-0
        1. Science--Miscellanea--Juvenile literature. [1. Plants--Miscellanea. 2. Questions and answers.] I. Title. II. Series.

    Q173 .T55 2001
    580--dc21

                                                                    2001023214

**Picture acknowledgements:**
Mark Bowler/NHPA: 22tr. Donna Disario/Stockmarket: 19t, 19cl, 19cr, 19b.Liz Eddison/Bruce Coleman: 20-1 background. ExtraEye: 21c.
O. Grunz/Powerstock Zefa: 13tl. Brian Henderson/Bruce Coleman: 21cr.
David Lawrence/Stockmarket: 21br. David Muench/Stone: 9t.
Powerstock Zefa/Index: 11 background. Hans Reinhard/Bruce Coleman:
23b, 24tr. Clyde H. Smith/Still Pictures: 18 background. Kim Taylor/Bruce
Coleman: 23cl. Roger Tidman/NHPA: 20tr. Juliette Wade/Garden PL:
25 background. J. Whitworth/A-Z Botanical PL: 22b.

All other photography by Ray Moller.

# Contents

# Why can't I grow a pebble?

Because pebbles are
not living things.

Only living things
such as plants, animals,
and people can grow.

Stones, metals, bricks,
and plastics are not
living things.

9

# Why are nuts so hard to open?

## Because they have a tough outer shell.

Nuts are seeds. A seed contains a tiny new plant and food to help it grow.

The tough outer shell protects this plant parcel until the seed is ready to sprout.

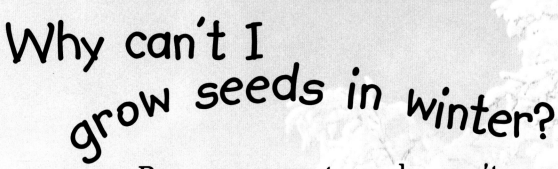

# Why can't I grow seeds in winter?

Because most seeds can't grow when it's very cold.

Seeds grow best in spring,
when the rain falls and
the sun warms the soil.
Rain makes the seeds swell.
Sunshine helps them to grow.

# Why can't I have lunch with my plant?

Because plants don't eat like we do.

Plants take in food
in a different way from people.
They are the only living things
that can make their own food
inside themselves.

All they need is sunlight,
air, water, and nutrients
from the soil.

12

# Why do plants need water?

## Because water helps them to stay alive.

Plants soak up water
through their roots.
The water moves up
through the stem
to the leaves.

The leaves use
some of the water
for making food.

# Why can't I keep my plant in the dark?

Because plants need light
to stay healthy and strong.

Plant leaves use sunlight to make food and
help them build their roots, stems, and leaves.

Plants cannot
make food
if they are kept
in the dark.

They grow weak
and their leaves
turn pale.

# Why can't I grow plants without *soil?*

Because most plants need soil to grow.

Soil holds water that the plant roots soak up. It also has nutrients in it.

Plants need these nutrients to grow strong and healthy.

# Why can't I take my plant for a walk?

Because plants have roots that hold them firmly in the soil.

Plants don't have to search for food. They can spend their whole lives rooted in one place.

Their roots stop them from falling over or blowing away in the wind.

# Why can't I push this tree over?

Because its roots are too deep, wide, and strong.

Trees are the biggest plants on earth. They can grow taller than a house.

Trees have a strong woody stem called a trunk and deep spreading roots.

Why don't many trees have leaves in winter?

Because leaves fall off in the fall, when the days become shorter and darker.

In the fall,
there is not enough
sunlight for leaves
to make food.

fall

When the leaves
can no longer work,
they die and
fall off.

summer

winter

spring

Then the tree rests
until next spring
when new leaves
start growing.

# Why can't I grow a pineapple in my garden?

## Because pineapples can grow only in hot places.

Different plants grow in different places. Cacti grow best in dry deserts. Waterlilies grow in muddy ponds. Fir trees grow on cold mountainsides.

cacti

waterlilies

fir trees

21

# Why can't I eat thistles?

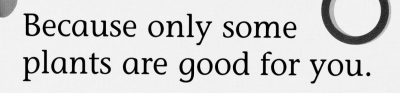

## Because only some plants are good for you.

Fruit and vegetables, grains, seeds, and nuts are good foods.

Thistles are too hairy and prickly to eat. Other plants are too bitter or poisonous.

# Why can't I pick nettles?

## Because they will sting you.

Plants cannot run away from animals that want to eat them.

Nettles have stinging hairs and other plants have prickles to protect themselves.

# Why can't I pick all kinds of wild flowers?

Because if everyone picked them, there would be none left.

Flowers make seeds,
so that new plants
can grow.
If you pick a flower,
it does not have
time to make seeds.

Without seeds,
no new flowers
can grow.

# Why can't I live without plants?

Because plants give us all sorts of things we need to live.

Plants give us food such as fruit and vegetables, bread, and pasta. They give us wood for buildings and fuel to keep us warm.

Plants make the air good to breathe.

# Plant words

**desert**  A very dry place where it hardly ever rains.

**flower**  The part of a plant that turns into fruit.

**fruit**  The part of a plant that holds seeds. People can eat sweet and juicy fruits.

**leaf**  Plants make food in their leaves.

**nut**  A fruit with a hard outer shell.

**root**  Roots hold a plant firmly in the soil. They also take in water for the plant.

**seed**  Most plants grow from seeds.

**soil**  The earth in which plants grow.

**stem**  The stem holds up the plant. It carries water and food to other parts of the plant.

**tree**  A type of plant that often grows to a big size. The largest single living thing on earth is a tree. Trees live longer than any other plants and some live longer than any animal.

# Can you find out what these phrases mean?

- a bed of roses
- weed out
- in a nutshell
- a hard nut to crack
- pear-shaped

- to put down roots
- to shake like a leaf
- as fresh as a daisy
- to spill the beans
- to bark up the wrong tree

# Do you know what these things are?

- a wallflower
- a bean-bag
- thistledown
- a tree-house
- a thorny problem

- a clinging vine
- a needle in a haystack
- rose-colored glasses
- leaf mold

# Think of another word to describe someone who is or has:

- weedy
- wooden
- a green thumb

- full of beans
- willowy
- rosy-cheeked

- nutty
- prickly
- up a tree

# Notes for parents and teachers

Read through this book with children, so that they become familiar with the ideas and words to do with plants. Then try the activities suggested below, to reinforce some of the ideas and give the children further talking points.

### Collecting seeds
Make a labeled collection of seeds to compare their shape, size, color, and texture. Wash and keep seeds from fruits and vegetables such as apples, oranges, alligator pears, and peaches. Raid your food cupboard for edible seeds such as rice grains, dried peas, beans, popcorn, sunflower seeds, and others. Spread out some bird food to see what seeds are used for this. Collect fruits and seeds from garden plants, such as dandelions and poppies. In the fall, search for acorns and cones that drop from pine trees.

### Good enough to eat
Lay out a variety of different vegetables and help children identify which parts of a plant these are. An interesting selection might include lettuce or spinach leaves, a root vegetable (such as a carrot, turnip, or parsnip), celery stalks, pea pods, tomatoes, and onions.

### What grows?
Try planting bird seed and some frozen peas. Scrape the mud from your boots into some compost. Does anything grow?

## Planting experiments

Soak some peas or broad beans for 24 hours and use them to try out a few experiments. Seeds vary, and some will grow better than others. Always use more than one seed in any experiment.

- Does it matter which way I plant a bean?
  Try planting three beans the right way up, three upside-down, and three horizontally.

- What happens when I cut a bean in half?
  Plant three whole beans in one pot and three half beans in another pot.

- Do beans need water?
  Plant three beans in one pot and three in another. Regularly water only one of the pots.

- Do beans need light?
  Plant three beans in one pot and three in another. Keep one pot in a cupboard.

- Does the soil type matter?
  Sow three seeds in pots with different types of soil—such as sand, clay, compost, a mixture of sand and soil, and garden soil. Talk about why their growth might differ.

## Plant scrapbook

Cut out pictures from brochures and magazines that show plants growing in different climates and environments and make a plant scrapbook. Talk about the reasons for why different kinds of plants grow in different places.

# Index